First Name BARBIE
Last Name DOLL

First Name BARBIE
Last Name DOLL

Maureen Bocka

HEADMISTRESS PRESS

Copyright © 2016 by Maureen Bocka.
All rights reserved.

ISBN-13: 978-0692604762
ISBN-10: 0692604766

This book may not be reproduced, in whole or in part, including illustrations, in any form (beyond that permitted by Sections 107 and 108 of the U.S. Copyright Law and except by reviewers for the public press), without written permission from the publishers.

Cover art © 2014 by Jessica Burke, *Angëlle as Faye Dunaway as Joan Crawford of Mommie Dearest*. Cover & book design by Mary Meriam.

PUBLISHER
Headmistress Press
60 Shipview Lane
Sequim, WA 98382
Telephone: 917-428-8312
Email: headmistresspress@gmail.com
Website: headmistresspress.blogspot.com

Contents

The Ghosts of my Barbies Speak Up	1
I Want to Love You	2
Malibu Barbie	3
Ballerina Performs for President	4
Tokidoki Barbie	5
Taylor Contemplates Ken	6
Soccer Barbie	7
Laundry Day Barbie	8
Imperfections	9
Orca Dreams	10
Sofi Addresses Admirer	11
Consummated Union on the Giant Bed	12
President Barbie's Future	13
Midnight's Princess	14
Surfer Gurl takes a Stand	15
Not for All the Pony Rides in the World	16
Shamu's Answer	17
President Barbie Concurs	18
Financially Unstable Barbies	19
Kelly Returns	20
Daisy's Imaginary Wedding	21
Love Lessons from Shamu	22
We Never Left	23
Margaret Reminisces about Loss	24
Salvaged Dolls	25
Acknowledgments	27
About the Author	28

The Ghosts of my Barbies Speak Up

Margaret and I were "friends," remember?
Went clubbing in space between bunk bed and single bed.
Pirouetted to Spice Girls songs.
Margaret would cuddle with me and her head
rest on my hard, hollow chest.

Then Ken, who fondled girls half his age
went after Margaret who could care less.
I hated him for it.
Stole away to G.I. Joe's Barbie wife.
She's my secret girlfriend. (Shh. Don't tell Margaret).

Whispered to her Ken's affair with Margaret
and Barbie managed to get Ken recruited.
Margaret never said another word about him.
We were left in the gentle hands of our girl child.

I Want to Love You

In college years President Barbie frequented bars.
Place where she met Surfer Gurl Barbie.
Tall, tan, Ken-sized feet and purple highlights.
Dominated all the sand volleyball competitors.
Could even take out metro Ken players.
She would dance on tables and get free drinks from admirers.

Once when Surfer Gurl needed a break she introduced herself.
Let's get some air.
Led her to the patio and began slow dancing.
Surfer Gurl liked being held by jointed arms and hands.
When the song was done President kissed Surfer Gurl's hand.
Please come home with me, whispered President.

I'm leaving for competition tomorrow, baby doll.
Thanks for a wonderful evening.
Walking home President replays the evening
over and over wondering if she had enough charm.
One day she will think of her and remember tonight.
At least she'll watch her on TV.

Malibu Barbie

Having hair brushed when SNAP!
Platinum hair now tangle free.
Only way to kill Barbie is amputate head.
Every doll loses her head every now and then.
Some even lose their limbs.

Pieces of her neck remain on desk.
Malibu is uncomfortable being played with.
It is disorienting having her body
picked up leaving her head behind.

Now she lies among pens and stress balls on the desk.
Fluorescent dress sparkles in lamplight.
Never again can she turn head and look.
This is the price to be reborn.

Ballerina Performs for President

Ballerina has always understood
you dance for the most important
person. Today that is President.
Let the audience know why
she has pink tiara on head.
Tour jetés, arabesques, and sous sus.
Ribs in, chin up, and smile.
Dazzle her with your finale:
left spilt arms in high fifth.
She is sweaty, breathing hard,
and grateful to do this every day.
After the show, President shakes hands.
"I understand why you are prima, Ballerina."
"Thank you Miss President."
She loves art so she cannot imagine
giving it up without a few tears.
Ballerina would never have to retire.
Barbies are ageless and immortal.
Ballerina could not give up dancing
even while considering moving
into the White House.

Tokidoki Barbie

She is bad ass covered in tattoos.
Real ones not wimpy temporary tats.
Tiger on neck distracts from her pink bob.
Remove her skull t-shirt
and see masterpiece on her back.
Mean dragon, lotus flowers,
and a butterfly grace her back.
On chest flowers, clouds, and heart with crown
that says "Tokidoki Mon Amour."
Even left arm is inked with geisha.
Is it any wonder that she is a limited edition?
No child will ever handle her.
Femme fatale fashion says *keep away*.
Leopard print leggings,
mini skirt, and glittery heels.
She deserves to be placed on a motorcycle.

Taylor Contemplates Ken

Taylor is also known as Locket Surprise Barbie.

Ellen said you don't need boys. That could be true.
There is nothing I want more than Ballerina
running hands through my hair.
Ken, sometimes I think our love affair was forced.
Gave me a ring and put your picture in my chest.
I am forever your locket.
What were your real intentions?
Lost ring and do not miss him.
Don't miss waiting around end table and being disappointed.
Sadly, he will be inside me and haunt forever.
I wonder what will happen with Ballerina.
I like it when Ballerina holds me in her lap.
Hey B, let's go dancing together and forget our exes.
I am not the kind of girl who does these things.

Soccer Barbie

In 1999 Barbie played in the FIFA World Cup.
She is really going to have to convince us.
Do soccer players really have brushes that match their uniforms?
I'm not sure her legs have ever been through a match.
Through unknown mechanics she can kick and throw.
Maybe she means business
there is a tiny bottle of Powerade behind her.
Mussed bangs surely mean Barbie can play hard.
Next to her in the box is a picture of Mia Hamm.
Barbie might be riding on Mia's credentials.

In 2013 Barbie played soccer as Soccer Barbie.
She officially is a glamazon.
Her legs have gotten even thinner,
but now she has knees and elbows.
The soccer ball, participation trophy,
and uniform are all nauseatingly pink.
This time she is alone.
Barbie is hardly an athlete.
She just doesn't do the Olympic Soccer team justice.
Is that Megan Rapinoe laughing?
Barbie is officially a spoof of herself.

Laundry Day Barbie

Ken you are a filthy man-whore.
You wanna rip my clothes off,
never offer to clean.
You throw suits, swim trunks, and jerseys
into my yellow laundry basket.

This isn't the freaking 1960's.
I'm a vet, doctor, astronaut, news reporter,
army ranger, and into infinity.
I have more careers than you do.
Would it really kill you to help me out?

Don't you dare say I'm bad at cleaning!
I'm not asking you to be President
or anything else out of your league.
Just do your part.
I'm overworked, underpaid, and this is old.

Imperfections

President Barbie holds in her hands
not only the future of Barbies in Barbieland,
but a blue crocodile.
He is beautiful in an odd way
with black and white stripes.
Smiling with one eye looking
forward one looking back.
His only purpose is to exist and delight a viewer.
President aware of overly long neck, legs, and arms.
Her torso impossibly narrow hidden with blazer.
Venus de Milo is the epitome of beauty
as Barbie is the all-American woman.

Orca Dreams

For 14 years of life
Shamu longed for Barbie friend
to play with her in water.
Annual voyages to Lake Michigan
with woman adult included
bobbing up and down to undulations,
diving under reappear covered with sea weed,
basking in sand castle moat.
What is it like to have Barbie sit on back?
Dreams of snout pat pulled by her fins.
Shamu sunbathes under bathroom window
on green towel waiting for companion.

Sofi Addresses Admirer
For Megan Bott

Sofi is a 1993 Mary Poppins Barbie.

You want to be like me?
Oh girlie, you know how to charm a doll.
It's because you met me with shoes.
Women like dolls to have shoes.
It means we have adventures.
True I never married, but my finger has a hole.
For years and years, I was stuffed in a pink backpack.
No way of knowing who was above or next to me.
All I wanted was to find my companion.
Oh, but don't you worry dear,
Daisy likes to take me to parties and
that makes for good distraction
especially when there's a princess.
I hope she kisses us straight on the lips.
I like boldness in my woman, otherwise
you might as well be dating shadow.
Still girlie, I cannot forgive you for wanting
hypothetical children to play with sticks and rocks.
You know you still love me.
Kiss kiss.

Consummated Union on the Giant Bed

I visit the first night of our union
after you have fallen asleep.
While gazing into eager green eyes
and noticing your wide shoulders
purple dress fell to ankles.
Lady Godiva is put to shame.
Blonde hair covered you like a blanket.
How is it we are meant for each other?
Your lips started on my lips
trailed my body.
Leaving kisses where they land.
Dress ourselves sleep on shelf.
Sleep on top of me.
I never want to wake without you.

President Barbie's Future

After term I want to move into a Frank Lloyd Wright house.
Free to do what I want with extra security.
Go to more of Ballerina's shows
or an Olympic sand volleyball game.
It is exhausting hiding imperfections.
Maybe I'll walk through the street
wearing nothing but pink wedges.
We can have all the sleep overs we want.
I want to party and let go.
Sofi can look after me.
Most of all I just want time to spend
with my partner Daisy.
She has earned a drive in the van and a vacation.
Perhaps we will go see the cacti in the living room.
I have another surprise for her
and this one she will not see coming.

Midnight's Princess

Rapunzel ran away from shelf
and climbed up the giant bed.
No idea where she was.
Tears fell down her cheeks.
How could Barbie have been so careless?
She shouldn't have kissed Ballerina.

Sat down by decorative pillow.
Did not know he is sneaking up on her.
What is that golden tassel thing?
He crouches, orange eyes focused.
Sniffs then flicks it with his paw.
Rapunzel tilts her head, wipes her eyes.

Midnight gives braid giant flick
lies flat on stomach.
She turns and sees Beanie Baby panther
trying to act like a kitten.
Sits up to show he can be regal, too.

Midnight nuzzles and Rapunzel hears rumbly purring.
He will not eat her, but licks her hand.
Tunnels under arm and puts felty nose on cheek.
"Will you come home with me?"
He bows his head and waits.
Rapunzel hikes up skirt
and sits on Midnight's back.
He gallops on pink blanket.
Adventure can be anything when you are a princess.

Surfer Gurl Takes a Stand

Popular in 1980's
tormented ever since.
Do not let my smile fool you.
What do you want from me?
You say my goal is corrupt youth.
I wanted to give them dreams
about their boundless potential.
Know it's ok to be more
than mom for plastic baby.
My body shamed in online articles
comparing me to "real" women.
Let me ask you a question:
Will you promise to leave me alone from now on?
I wish I could tell you my history.
Make you see past all the pink
distractions and see my life.
Hope scholars never make
lesbian Barbie discovery.
I could not stand to hear what they say.

Not For All the Pony Rides In the World

Margaret sat down at end of radiator
and put on "come hither" smile.
She waited for Tanya
to saddle brown and white pony.
Pony started trotting toward Margaret.
Every three steps
Tanya had to be helped back on.
As she watched
Margaret thought a tiny hand
was trying to hold hers.
Tanya dismounted and
sat down next to her partner.
Put her arm around Margaret's shoulders.
Turned her head and whispered,
I miss her, too.

Shamu's Answer

Shamu and her baby glide through purple water at Barbie Beach.
She remembers when she looked at toy catalogues
and wanted Ocean Friends Barbie.
Barbie could sit on Shamu's fin via Velcro.
Swimming is more fun with a companion.

Now Shamu watches sand volleyball team practice for Olympics.
Surfer Gurl cooled off in the lake to be nose to nose with Shamu.
Is this the mysterious whale I have heard about?
Shamu gave gentle whale call
and baby rested head on Surfer Gurl's calf.

Barbies are nothing to be scared of.
See how nice and calm she is?
Shamu smiled as her snout was petted.
After persistent nosing Surfer Gurl took a ride on Shamu's back.
Sometimes us dolls get more than we asked for.
Shamu sounds as though she is saying, "Thank you."

President Barbie Concurs

As a Barbie loving Barbie
I find it unacceptable humans
are allowed to dictate attractiveness.
My body does not match human anatomy.
Barbies descended from fashion paper dolls.
We were supposed to be easy for small girls.
Glad we only frustrate the childish adults!

Do not shame us.
First they blame us for being the
"ideal woman" and having "upper class" status.
We don't even have a Barbie mansion!
All 20 of us sat on an end table beneath a window.
We fought for every square inch of space.

If it's ever known my friends and I
are lesbians we'll be incinerated for sure.
There is still no universal acceptance for us.
I thought we showed girls the power of women.
I quickly found out it works both ways.
Live with us or without us.
Let it be clear we are never going away.

Financially Unstable Barbies

No mansion or castle.
Prime real estate means the black end table
pushed underneath the bedroom window.
We sit in three rows elbow to elbow.
Car pool together in pink van.
Do not have official pets
we took in a wild Beanie Baby panther
that roamed the bedroom at night.
Wear same clothes over and over.
No room for more anyway.
Where do you put clothes
if you do not have a closet?
Living within our means
freaks everyone out.
We were never advocates
for excessive luxury.
Our clothing has not been updated
since the 90's.
We do not invite Barbies
from across town to our parties.
We just want to be ourselves.

Kelly Returns

In my dream last night Kelly is on living room couch.
Cuddly pajamas and bath robe gone.
Puts her arms up to be held.
As her parents are gone I picked her up.

She was safe, warm, and loved.
Had you never been lost
to a girl who could not keep her word
I might be forgiven of losing
my dolls only child.

Your infinite girlhood is bizarre.
Never growing up has its consequences.
Is playing dress up any consolation
for never getting to live your dreams?

Sure you may want to be like Barbie,
but Kelly will always be Kelly.
Go back to your mothers Kelly.
You will not be here when I wake.

Daisy's Imaginary Wedding

Daisy is better known as Cut Style Barbie from 1994.

Courthouse weddings are convenient
when trying to outsmart press.
I wore my usual evening gown
and threw on a pair of purple heels to finish the look.

I'm more sophisticated than flashy.
My dear friend Sofi gave me a drink to relax.
She makes a good cocktail.
Skip over rings, our certificate is enough.

Other dolls give us enough respect.
I'm prepared for an adjustment period.
Especially when our marriage lives
in my imagination.

Too bad President Barbie does not believe in marriage.
I know better than to make her change her mind.
She could have been my wife.

I loved President Barbie.
All the van rides, VIP parties,
and talks in the moonlight were all for naught.
How was I supposed to know you would leave?

Love Lessons From Shamu

President decided to visit Olympic sand volleyball team.
Group of strong women is a welcome change
from grumpy politicians.
During practice she thought
if these women can spike a ball
what could they do to someone's nose?
Those fierce women
held onto femininity with both hands
while keeping aggressive front.
Pink and blue sunglasses are not enough
to distract from lunging legs and slapping the ball.
Coach blew her whistle,
twenty minute break.
After meeting team,
President asked Surfer Gurl
to show her the orcas.
Sure enough Shamu surfaced with baby
and chorus of orca calls began.
Shamu splashed Surfer Gurl.
President then understood
what it looks like to find someone
who loved before they had even met.

We Never Left

Tanya and I wanted a child.
One day Kelly came home to us.
She came in a pink and cardboard box
wearing a bath robe with a rubber ducky on it.
We adopted her. She looked just like me.
Tanya would give Kelly a bath in pink bathtub,
wrap her up in bathrobe and bring her to me.
We would tell stories and sing to her until bedtime.

Barbie and Ken also wanted to be parents.
I did not give Kelly up.
She split her time between both of us.
Then one day the girl child who lived
down the street "borrowed" Kelly.
Never saw her again.
I'm sorry Kelly.

Margaret Reminisces about Loss

Tanya and I redefined happiness.
We hid the bathtub among the giant rubber duckies
in the bathroom.
We would have coffee in silence some days.
Spent all the time we could together.
Then in 1997 our home in the basement
flooded and we drowned.

Yet you're still not over us.
You've held on to that lacy party dress of mine.
I am proud that Surfer Gurl wears it.
Goodness dear, you have no idea
how much I want to be there for you.

We would have loved to have been there
when you knew you were just like us.
Maybe we would have given you strength.
I always regret the fact that we left you so soon.

Past regrets cannot help you now.
Instead tell them how you would agonize
over what dress to put on us.
How tenderly you brushed our hair.
You were the only girl for us
and we thank you for that.

Salvaged Dolls

We all know what happens to Barbie
after her child friend grows up.
If she is lucky, she will be given away.
At flea markets she sunbathes
in a group of dolls on a blanket.
It is hard to tell if she has any friends or lovers.
At thrift shops she is put in plastic bags
with other dolls and miscellaneous toys.
Often Barbie has been stripped
of her clothes and her identity.
Who would they become?
There is nothing sexual about nudity
when it is part of the process
of finding a new home.
There are a few dresses that do not belong
to any doll in the pink back pack.
All rescued dolls need a disinfectant wipe and shampoo.
There are enough dolls at home.
No point trying to rationalize an attraction
to someone both repulsive
and despite her exaggerations
beautiful.

Acknowledgments

Thank you to Meagan Cass for your encouragement and for allowing me the freedom to write what interested me in your classes.

Thank you to Tracy Zeman for your mentorship and for all you wisdom. These poems shine because of you.

Thank you to my writing friends Erich O'Connor and Jacob Cross for all your support.

Thank you to Mary Meriam, Risa Denenberg, and Rita Mae Reese for believing in my poems and making them into something beautiful.

About the Author

Maureen Bocka is a recent graduate of University of Illinois Springfield. She has previously served as assistant managing editor of *The Alchemist Review* and *Uproot Magazine*. This is her first collection of poetry.

Headmistress Press Books

Lovely - Lesléa Newman
Teeth & Teeth - Robin Reagler
How Distant the City - Freesia McKee
Shopgirls - Marissa Higgins
Riddle - Diane Fortney
When She Woke She Was an Open Field - Hilary Brown
God With Us - Amy Lauren
A Crown of Violets - Renée Vivien tr. Samantha Pious
Fireworks in the Graveyard - Joy Ladin
Social Dance - Carolyn Boll
The Force of Gratitude - Janice Gould
Spine - Sarah Caulfield
Diatribe from the Library - Farrell Greenwald Brenner
Blind Girl Grunt - Constance Merritt
Acid and Tender - Jen Rouse
Beautiful Machinery - Wendy DeGroat
Odd Mercy - Gail Thomas
The Great Scissor Hunt - Jessica K. Hylton
A Bracelet of Honeybees - Lynn Strongin
Whirlwind @ Lesbos - Risa Denenberg
The Body's Alphabet - Ann Tweedy
First name Barbie last name Doll - Maureen Bocka
Heaven to Me - Abe Louise Young
Sticky - Carter Steinmann
Tiger Laughs When You Push - Ruth Lehrer
Night Ringing - Laura Foley
Paper Cranes - Dinah Dietrich
On Loving a Saudi Girl - Carina Yun
The Burn Poems - Lynn Strongin
I Carry My Mother - Lesléa Newman
Distant Music - Joan Annsfire
The Awful Suicidal Swans - Flower Conroy
Joy Street - Laura Foley
Chiaroscuro Kisses - G.L. Morrison
The Lillian Trilogy - Mary Meriam
Lady of the Moon - Amy Lowell, Lillian Faderman, Mary Meriam
Irresistible Sonnets - ed. Mary Meriam
Lavender Review - ed. Mary Meriam